DON'T
BURN
YOUR
TOAST

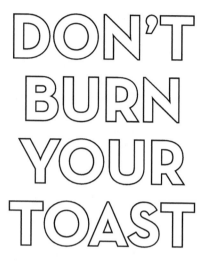

DON'T BURN YOUR TOAST

THE Guide to an Unforgettable Wedding Speech

Pete Honsberger

ARCHWAY
PUBLISHING

This book is a work of non-fiction. Unless otherwise noted, the author and the publisher make no explicit guarantees as to the accuracy of the information contained in this book and in some cases, names of people and places have been altered to protect their privacy.

Archway Publishing books may be ordered through booksellers or by contacting:

Archway Publishing
1663 Liberty Drive
Bloomington, IN 47403
www.archwaypublishing.com
1 (888) 242-5904

Because of the dynamic nature of the Internet, any web addresses or links contained in this book may have changed since publication and may no longer be valid. The views expressed in this work are solely those of the author and do not necessarily reflect the views of the publisher, and the publisher hereby disclaims any responsibility for them.

Any people depicted in stock imagery provided by Thinkstock are models, and such images are being used for illustrative purposes only. Certain stock imagery © Thinkstock.

ISBN: 978-1-4808-4474-2 (sc)
ISBN: 978-1-4808-4475-9 (hc)
ISBN: 978-1-4808-4476-6 (e)

Library of Congress Control Number: 2017905070

Print information available on the last page.

Archway Publishing rev. date: 4/13/2017

This book is dedicated to you,
who won't take this
honor and responsibility lightly.
Have some fun with it, too.

Contents

1

Introduction

Let me first say, congratulations Mr. Best Man or Ms. Maid of Honor! You officially can never again complain about nobody loving you because you were selected by your brother, sister, best friend, cousin, bold acquaintance, or weird, lonely co-worker to represent the most important peer in what will be one of the most important days of his or her life.

Let me next say…want to *hear* a good wedding speech?

Hop on YouTube and type in any combination of "Best speech," "Great wedding speech," "Best best-man speech" or "Maid of honor great speech." Some will be entertaining, and some will have Eleven thousand views for reasons that make about as much sense as a six-dollar handling charge on a twenty-dollar concert ticket that gets automatically emailed to you anyway. To be honest, it's not a terrible place to start for inspiration.

```
best best man|
```
best best man **speech**
best best man **gifts**
best best man **speech jokes**
best best man **toast**
best best man **quotes**
best best man **speech examples**
best best man **speeches of all time**
best best man **opening lines**
best best man **gifts ever**
best best man **speech for a brother**

Seriously, try the google search.

Kick back with a coffee, ice water or bourbon pour and struggle through the 30-second ads to take in some speech examples. I will tell you that the ones with the most views seem to be from Canadian weddings. If someone can explain that to me, I'm all ears. Truthfully, Internet research is better than no research at all. Watching videos, however, will not put pen to paper or words to Word Document for you. And to stand out in a crowd of average, forgettable speeches, you've got to put in your own work.

So…want to *create* a great wedding speech?

You've come to the right place. This is definitely where you parked your car. This book contains a path to a great wedding toast, down to the necessary components, questions to ask yourself, prompts to get you started, and a checklist to keep you on track. Research is part of the process, and hey, it's probably how you found this work of art known as *Don't Burn Your Toast*. Like it or not, your toast is a big deal and it deserves more time and attention than you would give a freshmen persuasive speech project.

With this great power comes great responsibility, the kind that puts Tobey Maguire [1](I mean Spiderman) to shame. Not only will your name be eternally embossed in the decorative wedding ceremony program and the reception table cards, but you will also have the pleasure (or horror) of planning a bachelor/bachelorette party that may require multiple trips to Spencer Gifts. Also, you'll get to put $1,000+ hotel deposits on your credit card!

Don't worry, though, most of the party's guests will pay you back for the villa suite, albeit months down the road. Also, there was no intended product placement or endorsement for Spencer Gifts, but that is subject to change if the fine store's representatives read this and want to bust out the sponsorship checkbook.

Pre-wedding festivities aside, the position you are in comes with the exciting and dreaded, anticipated yet feared, loved and hated responsibility of delivering a wedding toast as the best man or maid of honor.

---

[1] Tobey Maguire played Peter Parker in about 10 Spiderman movies.

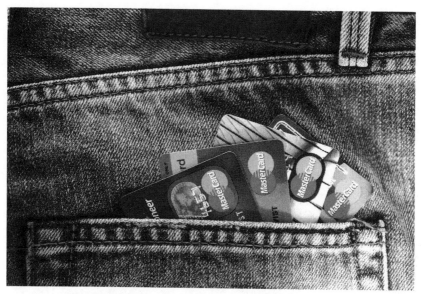

Credit cards are technically fake money, right?
So, really nothing to worry about.

"It's no big deal," some people might tell you. "Who cares? I wrote mine in five minutes and just winged it," you may also hear. If you wholeheartedly agree with these sentiments, then I'd recommended returning this book while you still have time. Get your money back, or take the store credit and get yourself some dishwasher detergent refills and a six-pack of thick paper towel rolls. Or, re-gift this sucker. Wrap it up at your next white elephant exchange and start a tradition where it changes hands every year during the holidays.

But if that's what you're selling, I'm not buying it. You've now taken the time to read the first 655 words of this book (that's an entire long blog article's worth of text), which tells me you have at least a little drop of curiosity about giving a better speech than ninety-five percent of the best man/maid of honor population.

On that note, here's the deal. I'm not here to disparage anyone that has already given a wedding toast or to say that yours will suck if you don't read and apply the concepts of this book. It probably will, but I'm not going to say it.

Honestly, as long as you're authentic and really care about your best friend, brother, sister or Craigslist guy that hired you to be the best man, your speech will be good enough to avoid lasting embarrassment.

But this book isn't for people interested in delivering a nightly news report speech that is heard tonight and forgotten by the morning. No, this book is for you, who wants to dig deeper into your vodka tonic and have people toasting so hard that glasses shatter throughout the room. This book is to make your speech memorable. This book is to help you pry laughs from the clutches of half-drunk, impatient guests while you stand between them and the re-opening of the bar. Most of all, this book is to give you the tools and practical advice so that you can honor, entertain and impact people that you care deeply about.

Doesn't look so hard from this angle, but wait 'til you get up there.

I'm writing this because of the times I've heard people recount cringe-worthy tales of wedding speeches. I think I can help. Look, I know none of this is life or death. If you bore a room for five minutes or break down and blubber through a disaster of a speech, life will go on. But my contention to you is that there's potential for your speech to be a tremendous opportunity that you embrace rather than a burden you dread. It should be a joyful time to honor someone that's so close to you and to deliver a tribute that truly does that person justice.

If I asked you to sum up your entire relationship with your best friend in five minutes, that's a daunting request. Now, imagine trying to do that off the cuff in front of two hundred people! All I'm saying is that this should be important to you, and if you really care, you'll have a plan and make it a point to do a great job.

I was in your shoes at least once. When my brother, Dan, asked me to give a toast at his wedding in 2011, I was incredibly excited. And really freaking nervous. So I did what I'm guessing most people do: procrastinate until the last week and then write the speech in a tiny notebook while I was getting an oil change. I don't know what it is about deadlines or pressure, but I tend to come up with my best stuff in the eleventh hour.

There's no better place to think than the body shop.

I remember sitting there, trying to produce a fresh idea while sketchy coffee with the powdered cream was sitting on top of the week's newspapers next to me. And as I scribbled down a few lines, an idea bolted into my mind and out poured the words. Next thing I knew, I had written an all-rhyming poem of a wedding toast that would both surprise the bride & groom and draw roars of laughter from the crowd. It worked out in this case, and that approach *might* work for some of you, too.

But it doesn't have to be like that. If you commit to finish this book three to four weeks before your wedding toast and follow the checkpoints included in the Dynamite Toast Checklist, you will cruise to the reception with a cool and confident demeanor. And best of all, you'll be ready to be memorable.

If there's one common theme that I want to drill into your mind like a railroad spike throughout out this book, it's that your speech, your audience, and the bride & groom deserve your best effort. A commitment to a small amount of consistent work is all it will take for you to knock this out of the park.

What I'm interested in is you eliciting GENUINE reactions to your speech, reactions similar to:

- "That was incredible!"
- "Amazing job! I didn't know half of those things about him (from the groom's mom)."
- "(Tears) …That was… (tears/blubbering) … so beautiful … thank you (more tears)."
- "Thank you for not doing a clichéd speech. That was a breath of fresh air."
- "Dammit, you nailed it. I was kind of afraid of what you might say, but that was perfect." (from the bride, groom, or their families)
- "I recorded the whole thing. It's going viral." (from a teenage cousin)
- "That was so awesome, tell me more about [insert story here]."
- "Don't forget us little people when you make it to Hollywood!"
- "The curtains are ON FIRE from that HEAT! Everybody out of the building, NOW!" (from the firefighters called to the scene because of your speech)

Without too much further ado, let's talk about how this book can help you burst into this speech to save the day like the Tyrannosaurus Rex at the end of *Jurassic Park*. No, not *The Lost World* or *Jurassic World*, I'm talking about the first one. You have to love the effort from T-Rex at the end of *Jurassic World*, too, but let's face it, he was outclassed by the Indominus Rex. I mean, how could he compete with a genetically modified beast that is part T-Rex, part velociraptor and part tree frog? That's why Big T needed some help at the end to survive.

Dinosaurs.

Just like you. You could fight this on your own, lock yourself in a dark room and write your speech. But if you truly want to succeed, enlist the help of this book and your loved ones (like the velociraptor and huge sea monster dinosaur) to survive and thrive.

See what I did there? That was inception.

2

Pains/Challenges

For the Boys

Alright guys, your brother, cousin or best friend calls you up. "I'm going to propose to Kelly, OMG, OMG, ZOMG!" First of all, please don't talk like that. Second, you start to wonder if you'll be the best man. A few weeks later, he calls and invites you to hang out at his place. When you're there, he pops the next question: "Will you be my best man?" This is great news!

How do you feel? You're probably excited, then honored, then soon after a sense of responsibility wafts over you like 315 lbs. resting on your shoulders at the squat rack. *Holy shit*, you think. *This means I have to plan the bachelor party, be the face of the groomsmen, and uh oh, give the best man toast.*

Let's be honest here in saying that this challenge is a good thing and, compared to real problems, is nothing. That doesn't mean it's easy, though. All of a sudden, you (who may not particularly enjoy speaking in front of more than three people) will soon be standing in front of two hundred guests with their eyes fixed upon you.

For the Ladies

Ladies, your sister, sorority little, former teammate, cousin, or best friend forever (BFF) shows up at your place with a gift bag. "First of all," she says, "thank you so much for being at my engagement. It means the world that you were there when Patrick proposed!" Meanwhile, she's handing you a bag full of lotions and potpourri[2]. "Obviously I want you to be one of my bridesmaids, but I'm here to ask you something else. Will you be my maid of honor?"

Now that's a gift bag.

After the hugging, tears (I'm not a woman so I'm taking some assumptive liberties here), spontaneous two-person flash mob, and half-bottle of champagne that you had hanging on an IKEA or

[2] This is probably not accurate ☺

Crate&Barrel wine rack (more product placement potential, who wants it?), you both sit down and catch your breath. Then the conversation turns to the wedding, which the bride-to-be has almost entirely planned in her head even though the engagement was a week ago. After the talk about the bachelorette party, the reception centerpieces, and dress shopping begins to subside, you're left wondering how you'll honor your friend with an unforgettable toast.

Regardless of who you are and your level of writing skill or speaking competency, giving this speech will be intimidating. I've been there. I've seen some very good and a lot of very bad. No, my experience will never be exactly the same as yours or anyone else's, but the similarities I see in the finished product across weddings are striking.

Here are some challenges you may encounter that deserve some advanced thought:

- **Being heard clearly by the audience**: Microphones aren't always clear, acoustics in the room may be a challenge, and it's easy to fall into a trap of either swallowing the mic or holding it somewhere near your belly button so only the first table can hear you.
- **Lighting in the room**: Will you be in an area where people can see you? Will there be a spotlight directly on you? That can be bright and uncomfortably warm.
- **Restlessness of the crowd**: If the bride or groom has little siblings or rowdy friends, you may have an uphill battle keeping these people's attention (and getting them to shut up).
- **Following another great speech**: If this is the case, you have about thirty seconds to get the audience to forget that person and focus on you. You've got to capture their attention and steer it completely away from the last speaker.

If you suck it up and finish this book, the challenge that may now be giving you anxiety will turn into a fun opportunity. Your speech will ignite you, not fill you up with carbon monoxide until you pass out.

3

It's Personal

For your sake and mine, I'll now be abbreviating the object of your speech to your BSF, which stands for brother, sister or friend. In most cases, your best man or maid of honor will fall within one of these categories. Before you start hollering, your cousin can also be your friend!

Now let's get back to why your participation in the wedding process is so special. It's why you see tears during the vows, misty eyes during the first dance, and elation on the bridal party bus. It's why the bride and groom's parents host parties, meals, and people at their residences the weekend of a wedding. It's why kids in their twenties and thirties spend an average of more than $20,000 for a one-day event. And it's the same reason why you spend the time to reminisce with old friends and make new ones: Time spent with loved ones.

What could be more personal than your relationship with a loved one? In your case, we're not talking about intimacy or romantic love (hopefully), but instead a chance to share a side of your BSF that most people in the room don't know, at least not in detail.

So many stories about this, mostly related to lack of sleep.

And, to me, the window that you can open to the audience about your BSF is why your speech is important in the first place.

This person has chosen you, out of the 7,000,000,000 people on planet Earth, as the best man or maid of honor. Because of the nature of your relationship with your BSF, you have a unique perspective and stories to tell. Who else knows the details of the seventh grade dance that produced photos of you both that would make today's fashion gods strike down on you with fury? Who else can tell a story about trading baseball cards with your brother and how he was awarded a valuable card because he knew the answer to the question, "When was the War of 1812," and you didn't? That actually happened to my brother and me—not my proudest moment. And while we're at it, who else knows the minute-by-minute details of when your BSF met the love of his or her life?

Can you tell an audience, some of whom are probably already half in the bag, everything about your BSF in a 10-minute speech? Of course not. Can you share two to three compelling tidbits about his or her life that show multiple facets of your dynamic friend? Hell yes you can, and you should!

Your advantage here is that you possess knowledge about this person that either nobody else or very few others have. Your disadvantage is that you can't talk to this audience like you would to your BSF. You can't make the speech in the special language the two of you have created using your own slang. If you do that, ninety-nine percent of the crowd won't get it.

At first thought, you may not care. Then again, the people in the room are important enough that the bride and groom (or bride and bride, groom and groom—you get the idea, right?) have spent tens of thousands of dollars to have them in attendance. So respect the audience by connecting them with some of your personal experiences involving your BSF.

If you can successfully engage the audience in the life of your BSF and the significant other, you give them opportunity to better relate to the two lovebirds, as well as everyone else in the room. The result is a stronger sense of community in the room.

Here's what I mean: The casual attendee or relative probably walks into the reception with plans to talk with friends and family that he or she already knows. Then your speech blows the doors off the place with stories of interesting facts about your BSF and his or her significant other.

Now, wait a minute. The casual attendee becomes curious to learn more. He or she may approach acquaintances to ask about stories in the speech. He or she may also be able to better visualize what the other family is like. Perhaps there are even similarities to explore and discuss between this casual attendee and the other family. Suddenly, it isn't as much a groom-side v. bride-side reception.

Don't hold me to this, but I believe this chain of events can lead to a more cohesive dance floor when the DJ starts spinning. Have you ever seen several dozen people, some who are complete strangers, singing *Purple Rain* in unison with locked arms?

I have. And it's f**king beautiful.

Breakfast can wait.[3]

To recap: If this chapter brings you any value, it should be in these two discoveries:

1. You know things about your BSF that almost everyone else doesn't. Leverage them to give people a glimpse into his or her personal life and engage people emotionally.
2. Find a way to deliver this personal information in a manner that the audience can understand and get excited about. You can keep a fraction of the slang or inside jokes, as this will add

---

[3] *The Chappelle Show* episode about Prince is one of the best ever.

PETE HONSBERGER

to the intrigue, but only a small fraction. The casual listener must be able to resonate with what you're saying for the impact to land.

You're part archeologist and part translator for the audience. To do this right, you'll be digging up golden artifacts about your BSF and delivering them to an excited crowd in a language they understand.

Get out your brushes, headlamp and Indiana Jones hat, and get to work.

Formulas

Math!

The best formula, or "structure," to your speech is completely subjective, of course. An attempt to tell you what you should do or need to do would be like me going to Nashville and telling musicians that they need to stop playing country because it isn't good. "Hey, buddy, take off those boots and switch to punk rock because that's the best kind of music." It sounds just as dumb typing it as it would be saying to someone's face.

But here's what I can tell you. There are structures to wedding toasts that are memorable to me, some that have made me cringe, and others of which I have absolutely no recollection.

Here are a few formulas I would avoid if I were you.

NO

1. Nervously laugh + Read straight from your phone + Stumble over words

2. Your overly critical story of when they met + List of things the groom better watch out for + Awkward and abrupt ending

3. Get hammered drunk + Apologize for being drunk + Unintentionally say something to offend the bride/groom and audience

4. Act too confidently + Tell stories that don't belong in a room of 200 people + Ignore the bride and/or groom

5. Rush the beginning because you're a mixture of nervous and happy + Start crying + Remain nearly inaudible for the remainder of the speech due to crying

6. Wait until the day before + Write three bullet points + Just wing it, because, "Whatever brah, open bar!"

7. Spend the whole speech on only the bride or groom + Look directly at your notes the whole time + Add disingenuous "welcome to the family" comment at the end

I'm confident that most of you wouldn't consciously choose to stumble over your words, offend folks in the audience, or ignore one of the two people getting married, but the truth is that I've seen people do these things. Whether because they are ill-prepared, going into panic-mode, or misjudging their surroundings, a lot of good people give bad speeches.

Ninety-five percent of the time, the difference between smiling success and withering embarrassment is a matter of about three hours of preparation and a couple practice runs in front of the mirror or your favorite mannequin. The other five percent of people need an intensive course just to bring themselves to the point of acceptable when it comes to public speaking. Maybe they're severely introverted, terribly shy in public, or just not fans of writing.

But take my exact percentages with a grain of salt. I'm not an analytics guy[4].

Now, let's explore some winning formulas. To be clear, I'm relaying speech structures that I have personally done, seen or heard from friends and family. If one of these is followed, you'll be equipped with the ammunition for a successful wedding speech experience.

If you commit yourself to it, this stuff will work. And by "commit yourself," all I mean is spending a few focused hours with the end goal in mind.

Take it away there Spartacus[5].

---

[4] I'm a Sabermetrics guy. Follow @PFTcommenter and @trillballins for more Sabermetrics

[5] If you don't recognize this reference, you've got to see the movie *That Thing You Do* immediately

YES

1. Brief story of when you met your BSF + Funny anecdote from your days together + A few things you like about the significant other + Closing joke to finish strong

2. Meaningful story of your reaction when your BSF asked you to be the best man/maid of honor + Best and worst (light-hearted or self-deprecating only) memory with your BSF + Things you have in common with the significant other + Heartfelt ending with toast

3. Killer opening joke/comedy bit + Meaningful compliments to the bride and groom (or bride and bride, groom and groom—no judgment here) + Shout out to your BSF's family + Ending joke that ties in with the opener

4. Soft opener that's respectfully building towards a story + #1 favorite memory of you and your BSF together + 1-2 things you and this person have done to annoy each other (keep it light) + The positive impact that the significant other has had on your BSF + Guide to a successful relationship with your BSF + One-liner to finish (sum up your BSF in 25 words or less)

5. Recite a quote, poem, or SHORT story that is relevant and interesting + Why it means something to you in the context of this wedding + Personal account of your history with your BSF + Wrap up with the Top 5 things you like about the significant other

6. Ask a question (i.e. How do I tell these two people how I really feel in 10 minutes or less?) + Answer that question many times throughout the speech keeping it as a common thread + Share what it was like when the significant other came into your BSF's life + From your perspective, share what they have to look forward to together

7. Start with a few childhood stories + Bring in a guest speaker (close friend or relative) for an appearance, keeping it short + Acknowledge the positive changes you've seen in your BSF since he or she has met the significant other + Finish sentimental to complete the journey from roaring laughter to dusty eyes

8. Start with the significant other (what is it about this person that you like, why he/she appeals to your BSF, your first impression and how that has changed, how he/she swept your BSF off her feet, etc.) + Move to your BSF and a brief timeline of your relationship + Transition to the families and give thanks

9. Make the whole damn thing into a poem

10. Some variation of these formulas, mixing and matching the components. However, it is important that you don't ignore any of the CRUCIAL COGS of the speech, which we'll be covering in Chapter 6.

Use these as prompts to get you started. Think about your life, your situation, and your relationships before choosing a formula. Or, move things around to fit with what you want your toast to accomplish. Just don't go rogue on me.

PETE HONSBERGER

5

For Starters

"Refuse to be held back by the fear of failure, or the fear of anything."

I think about that quote a lot. I'm not even sure where I heard it. But I think the sentiment is perfect for this book, and for any self-help efforts.

My guess is that a strong percentage of people who buy, borrow or steal this book to read it will do so out of fear. Fear of trying to write a good speech. Fear of being in the spotlight. Fear of failing during an important moment in a wedding celebration.

You're not alone. I have two major fears with every project. Starting and finishing them. I crush it in the middle, but it's always a challenge to figure out where to start. If you're like me, you may want to explore a bunch of angles first, write down ten different ideas or watch a dozen YouTube videos. I've got no beef with those as your initial approaches.

However, don't delay action until you think you have the perfect opening lines. I'm telling you right now, cut that shit out. When you're in this stage of the toast, quantity is more important that quality. The more you agonize over the perfect words or phrases, the less action you will take. The more you can face that fear and overcome it, the better your speech will be. I challenge you to use this book, mark it up, jot down ideas, and make notes in the provided pages in the back. Think but don't overthink. Just GO.

Remember the wise words of Vince Vaughn in the movie, *The*

Break-Up. Jennifer Aniston's character asks for help setting the table before a dinner party while Vaughn's character, "Gary," is watching television. Keep in mind she has already cleaned the condo and cooked the entire meal. His reply to her is

> You've done such a great job already, don't you want to finish it yourself and have that personal power, that accomplishment? Listen to me, do you think that when Michelangelo, right, was painting the 16th chapel, that he said 'hey guys I did pretty good on the first 15 chapels, but why don't you help me design this one? And maybe you could help me, grab me a brush and you guys can all grab brushes and we can make a great chapel?' Uh uh, no he didn't. And you want to know what the results were? A masterpiece!

The lesson I took from that brilliant and totally educated take is to paint all 16 chapels. Stopping after one, two, eight, nine, or even 15 won't cut it. Also, let's not worry about the fact that it's the Sistine Chapel, not 16 chapels. Just a minor detail.

Later in the book, I provide a step-by-step checklist for writing and executing a dynamite speech (with all 16 chapels), but for right now let the following sentiment cement itself in your brain: Treat this as an opportunity you anticipate more than a burden that you fear, and you'll free yourself up for success. Start your process with the right mindset. Get positive, get out your pen or laptop, and read on.

Looks like 16 chapels to me.

6

The Five CRUCIAL COGS

Cogs.

Note: If you're skipping ahead or picking chapters at random, this is a reminder that brother, sister, or friend has been abbreviated to BSF to save reading time and paper space. This small effort to go green just may save the world.

Merriam-Webster's [6]online dictionary defines "cog" as "a tooth on the rim of a wheel or gear," as well as "a subordinate but integral person or part."

For a wheel to work, its cogs must fit together and be turning in unison. I really like the word "integral" in the second definition. Without every cog doing its job, the wheel will not turn. Think about this in context of your wedding toast. Surely, there must be non-negotiable parts of your speech, right?

I mean, you've got to talk about your BSF. If you miss that part, you may as well not show up to the wedding. Then, think about the audience. They want to hear stories or anecdotes about the bride and groom. The audience wants to learn a little bit more about them as people, about their relationship, and about the people close to them. The audience wants to know that you value the significant other.

Heck, half the crowd is there because of the significant other, so you better not leave him or her out. Lastly, to give the people what they want you'll need to intrigue them from the start and send them to their glass-raising toast on a high note.

These pieces of a wedding speech can be simplified into five components that you absolutely need if you want to deliver an entertaining, meaningful and memorable toast. I'm calling them The Five CRUCIAL COGS because it sounds even more important, and maybe I can trademark the phrase and make some extra money from t-shirt sales. And there's also a tie-in because cogs are part of a wheel, which is a circular object that goes on forever. Like, say, the eternally circular symbol of a wedding ring? Whatever. Don't act like you wouldn't walk around with a CRUCIAL COGS message ironed on across your chest.

1. **The Opener:** For example: A funny or memorable story, quote, or memory of you and your sister. When you think about her, what first comes to mind? Make sure this is interesting so that it intrigues the audience.

---

[6] Definition retrieved from merriam-webster.com

2. **Honoring the Past:** When you think hard, which stories come to mind from when you were kids?

3. **Present and Future:** This could be related to a time when you went partying together, when she moved away from home, when you met the groom, etc.

4. **The Significant Other:** Don't forget to talk briefly about her brand new husband. Were you there when they met, what do you like most about him, what does he need to know about her, what should he do to avoid pissing her off, etc.?

5. **The Big Finish:** I love speeches that end on a high note with a joke, a quote, or some sort of grand sendoff message. This can be a dramatic display, emotional reading, or deadpan delivery. As long as you make it big, you'll be great.

Now, there is *some* room for improvisation within the Five CRUCIAL COGS, but I'm telling you that the farther you veer away from them, the higher your risk of failure becomes. They are directly correlated.

You may think these parameters will hold you back in some way, but as former Navy SEAL Jocko Willink tells us in his book, *Extreme Ownership*, discipline is freedom. Whether in sports, business, teaching or giving a speech, only after you have the fundamentals mastered can you innovate and test the boundaries.

In college, my football team had a defensive player named Scott who fascinated me. He would dance around before the ball was snapped (or hiked) and fake like he would blitz the quarterback. Then, at the last minute he would run back into the correct position, sometimes twenty or thirty yards away. This behavior was to throw off the opposing quarterback and offensive players so that they got nervous about his intentions during the play, potentially making a mistake as a result.

After watching this for a while, the wide-eyed freshman tenth-string player that I was asked him how he could get away with it. He told me that he knows where he needs to be like the back of his hand, and the coaches trust him to make all these moves because they know he will eventually end up in the right spot.

Pictured: An intimidating presence.

If that elaborate analogy doesn't work for you, try this one. By the way, if you think this is pandering, I apologize. Believe me I've already thought about that. If my analogies miss, they're going down in a blaze of glory.

Imagine you want to be a hairstylist and you want to be both creative and revolutionary. You have plans for new styles, coloring and methods that nobody else is doing. The concept you've designed includes varying lengths around a person's head, with shapes and designs that are extreme and yet still appropriate for most professionals to wear to work. You think you've found a way to service all of the people who want to try something new with their hair but are afraid of what their boss would say about it. I can tell you that I'm already interested in this service.

However, for as many drawings that you create, visions you dictate to friends and family, and predictions you make about your new company, none of it matters if you don't know how to cut hair. Before you can make this dream possible, you need to know your way around hair clippers and a pair of scissors. You need to know about hair in general, its makeup, the natural parts that allow for cutting, etc.

If you open a salon with great ideas but cannot demonstrate that you won't send me home looking a mutant, I can't take that chance. When you have the fundamentals down and they become second nature, only then I will sit in your chair and let you go to town. At that point, shave one side of my head, give me designs, or hook me up with the "everything" cut.

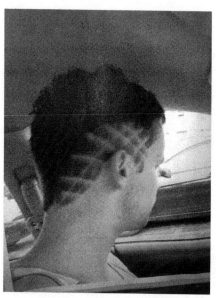

Something like this, perhaps.

After all this, the point is that taking the fundamentals (in this case, the Five CRUCIAL COGS) seriously will build a great foundation for your speech and open the door for additional ideas, jokes and fun. When we have the fundamentals nailed, only then can we be free to innovate.

So why are these CRUCIAL COGS presented in this order? Well, if you can grab the audience's attention and interest with an opening line or story, make allusions to the past and present with your BSF, show respect and love for the significant other, and finish strong, your toast will be a complete story. And it will be glorious.

You may even be asked for autographs afterward.

7

The Opener

Bang.

That's what you want to hear at the end of your first thirty seconds up there. It takes many forms but you'll know when it happens, if it happens. The bang is a gasp from the crowd, an eruption of laughter, the palpable feeling of the crowd's complete and undivided attention directed toward you.

This won't happen if you stumble through the first half-minute explaining who you are. It won't happen by scrolling through your cell phone, pausing to squint as you stare at the device instead of your audience. It won't happen if you are already tuned up (or *turnt up*) from Long Island Ice Teas and can't put a coherent sentence together. And it won't happen if you're reading from a bulleted list after you've convinced yourself that you'll just write down a couple main points and "figure out the rest" in the moment.

It WILL happen if you have prepared with one of your genuinely favorite memories of your BSF, especially if it's something that only the two of you know about. It will happen if you're able to capture the essence of your friendship in a quote, book excerpt, movie quote or shared interest. It will happen if you wait until you have the attention of the whole room, speak clearly into the microphone, and slowly pan your eyes across the reception hall in an excited, confident way. It will happen if you carefully and thoroughly prepare for your first thirty seconds, scripting every word and practicing it in the mirror or to your dog.

Here are a few examples of openers that I have personally used. I think they were effective, though the funny thing about speeches is their subjective nature. You may actually read this part and think you can do way better. To that, I would say "Do It!"

> Good evening everyone. I am Dan's younger brother Pete. Many of you I already know, some I have yet to meet. Dan and Kate, thank you so much for the chance to speak on this very special occasion…By the way, I call first dance. I've looked up to Dan ever since I've had sight. He was always bigger than me, and he was always right. Being the oldest of four boys couldn't have been an easy thing. But in a house full of hyenas, Dan was the lion king.

That particular opener happened to be a part of an all-rhyming speech. Remember, the idea just came to me while I was getting my oil changed. What I like about it is that it positioned me as knowing exactly what I was going to say from the very beginning. After the first two lines rhymed, the audience probably thought it was either a coincidence or the start of a poem. The latter was true.

Now, I had people hanging on the next line to hear what I had to say, or how I would go about fitting each line together according to the flow. I don't know if you like this approach at all. In fact, you may think it's downright stupid. But I can tell you with certainty that I had the attention of the room.

This is how that one ended.

Here's another opener from a speech that actually never saw the light of day, other than inside the card I sent to my best friend. He probably knew that I wouldn't be able to resist writing a speech for him and his wife, even if I didn't give the toast at his reception.

> Good evening ladies and gentlemen, my name is Pete Honsberger and I've been 'friend of' Brian for more than twenty years. And as I was preparing this, one question consistently rung in my mind…how do I summarize a friendship that has lasted since we were in kindergarten – believe it or not, Brian was under six feet tall then – but how can I possibly speak to all of our experiences in just a few minutes without it turning into one big inside joke?

While a more traditional approach, it contained two elements that set me up for success. First, I addressed head-on that I would not be turning the whole speech into an inside joke. Rather, I would be speaking to the crowd in a way that they could still enjoy. This was not going to be a turn-off for everyone outside our small circle of close friends.

Second, I posed a question that I would spend the rest of the speech trying to answer. To paraphrase myself, I pondered aloud how I would deliver a speech that does our friendship justice while still entertaining others in the room. My next several paragraphs were a mix of stories, anecdotes and a timeline of our friendship, told mainly as answers or ponderings directly related to that first question.

These examples are neither complete nor perfect. What they do, however, is wet the beak of the crowd and require them to perk up in order to be "in on the fun" for the duration of the toast.

Whether a loud, quick bang or a long train horn is more your style, the opener is the place to make that happen. All it requires is some thought, maybe some discussion, and of course, some auto body shop coffee (Baileys optional).

And the payoff is huge. The last thing you want is people sneaking off to the hotel bar to buy tequila shots halfway through your speech, accidentally slamming the door on their way out.

Honoring the Past

The past can be really nostalgic. What?
No I'm not, there's something in my eye.

Everyone has slightly unique shared experiences with their friends
and loved ones. However, based on dozens of weddings of personal

research, I have noticed that a few common themes of the past tend to appear. These are situations that become cornerstones of one's childhood, existing as fundamental building blocks to who we have become. While I would certainly encourage you to think outside of these if you have the memories and inspiration, the following themes can serve as a foundational soil from which your speech's stories grow. Use these as the car's frame while you are the engine that takes this thing through the road less-traveled to the finish line, miles ahead of almost everyone else. Here are a few pieces of the chassis:

- **Fondest memories involving both of you**: What sticks out?
- **Mischief**: What are things you did together that got you in trouble?
- **Fights/Battles**: When did you get under each other's skin? Is any of that humorous or worth sharing?
- **Vacation/Trip together**: Was there something that stood out? Did a defining moment of your relationship occur during one of these trips?
- **Growing pains**: Was there anything noteworthy about either of you, in terms of simply growing up? Did one of you have a fear of the opposite sex while the other was confident? Did one of you grow seven inches taller in a year?
- **Location-specific anecdotes**: Was there a memorable tree-house, friend's basement, swimming pool, school classroom, or school dance that produced vivid memories?

This should get you started. And though my official company line is to recommend you share two to three of these memories in your toast, you can do whatever you want. If you have a dozen one-liners about your past, by all means, rattle them off instead of two longer stories. But heed the warning that if you're just getting warmed up on your speech seven minutes into it, you will begin to hear the noise of people shifting in their chairs. That sound begins the sequence of wearing out your welcome.

The main idea of this COG is to provide depth into the person that is getting married. It's so subtle that it often goes unnoticed, but your characterization of your BSF as an interesting and curious person with an exciting past achieves a stroke of credibility with both his/her own family members, and more importantly, the significant other's.

Present and Future

How do you feel about this person now? What was your reaction when he/she asked you to serve this special role in his/her life? Where do you see your relationship with this person heading? In a light way, how will your interactions with your BSF shift now that there's a new number one in town?

These are all questions that deserve some thought *before* the speech, and honestly, some discussion with your BSF prior to the wedding. In broader context, I truly believe that honest exploration and discussion of these real-life issues leads to healthier and more rewarding relationships with our friends and family members.

Think about your top three best friends (a sister, brother, or cousin can count, too) that have gotten married. Ever since they got serious with their future husbands/wives, you have seen them less than before, right?

I bet you didn't know this book would offer friendship advice. Well, you probably also didn't know that Patty Hewes tried to kill Ellen Parsons in Season One of *Damages* (spoiler alert), but here we are. You don't even have to pay extra for this segment of the book.

If you've gotten married, are engaged, or plan to tie the knot anytime soon, please understand that your relationships have already been somewhat changed with your friends. You now have a #1 in your life, whereas you likely used to view your best friend or group of friends as the most important people in your world. If you understand this reality, you can consciously choose to make an effort to talk to and see your close friends. Do not fall off the face of the Earth. It gets exponentially harder to see everyone, but it's well worth it—for your own happiness and the happiness of those who care about you.

The Significant Other

This person is f**king special and incredibly important to your speech.

If that sounds harsh, it's because I don't want you to forget. It's too important.

Probably about ninety percent of the time, this person is beloved by you and your friends. Even if that's not entirely true, you better spend at least a minute of your speech celebrating the significant other. When I was trying to think of what to say about my brother's wife, Kate, I asked myself the following questions:

- How did they meet?
- Have she and I had any memorable interactions?
- Do they have any inside jokes that I'm aware of?
- What kinds of things is she into?
- Does Dan (my brother) do anything that annoys her? That was a pretty easy "yes." He hums when he eats. Been doing it for years. Also, he uses bread to sweep up any sauce or oil left on his plate during a meal. I don't knock his hustle at all, but I can see how it's viewed as disgusting by the rest of the world.

Of course, there are a host of other questions about the significant other that you can use as a spark for this segment of your toast. But now you at least have a *taste* of the thought-process. The main thing to remember about the significant other is that, to respect this person, you must examine your relationship with him or her and celebrate it.

Transitioning to the S.O.

It's definitely debatable which segment of your speech is the most important, but I'll tell you what's NOT the least important, and that's tastefully transitioning to the significant other and his/her family. The key to doing this well is striking the right balance between humor, intrigue and respectfulness. If the mention of the significant other is cliché and bland, it will come off as boring, forgettable, or worse, insincere. However, if you belly flop into this portion of the speech by mentioning, say, the "hotness" of the bride or the "stupidity" of the groom, you are in for an awkward next few days.

Here's a brief list of **Do's** when mentioning the significant other in your speech:

- The first thing your BSF told you about the significant other
- Something funny, non-threatening and quirky that the bride and groom share together (both love the same movie, neither can cook, they root for rival sports teams, etc.)
- Keep it relatively brief while still showing some love. A ten minute soliloquy[7] about the significant other will probably end up doing more harm than good. Nobody wants the best man or maid of honor to be too obsessed with the significant other.
- Share examples of how the significant other can "keep up" with you, your friends, or your BSF's family. Things like how she can party later than your buddies, how he turned out to be better at Charades than any of your squad, or how he'll go toe-to-toe with her parents on the topic of politics (respectfully, of course). This stuff can be hilarious.

---

[7] Thanks for the word Bill Shakespeare!

- Provide a short guide, or top five, to a successful life with your BSF. This can be both funny and meaningful.

And, of course, **Don't** mention the following things, unless you never want to see your friend again. Is that a threat? Insert big-eyeballs emoji here.

As a side note, I wanted to include a picture of Steve Buscemi's character from *The Wedding Singer* at this point in the book, but I don't want him coming after me. His character, Dave Veltri, was the epitome of what *not* to do during a best man speech. Even if it was legal to use his picture, I want no part of a potential feud with Steve Buscemi. Sorry folks, you'll have to use your imagination. Oh, and don't mention these things in your toast:

- Your first impression of the significant other if it was negative
- Anything that you think is weird or "off" about him/her
- A family quirk about the significant other (i.e. his uncle is a conspiracy theorist, her cousin is in prison, her dad doesn't know about her tattoos, etc.)
- Anything remotely related to your opinion of the significant other's attractiveness. If the world's ending on Monday, by all means, spout off about how when you first met Craig, you were like "He's really nice but I seriously thought Rachel could have done better." If not, step away from that line of speech.

Prepping the S.O.

Oh boy. I've seen a need for this once or twice.

As we've been over in detail, a wedding day is arguably the most important day of the bride and groom's life, unless one of them previously won the lottery, appeared on *The Voice*, or met a Jonas Brother. Kidding. But after all of the money, planning, frustrations, seat assignments, fittings, tastings, and rehearsals, they want the day to be perfect. So putting myself in their shoes here, I can imagine a scenario where the bride and/or groom are very concerned about what may be said in a speech.

I have also become privy on a few occasions to intel that suggested the bride and/or groom had warned the best man/maid of honor about their speeches (no names, please). While this initially seemed outrageous to me—how can you possibly have the nerve to censor someone's toast? —the more I thought about it, the more I get it. An incendiary line in the toast, hurtful shots at someone's family, or excessive stories of drunken stupidity can cast an unnecessary shadow on the evening.

While a fleeting bit of discomfort by the audience can make the rest of a toast even more funny, walking to the line of appropriateness, spitting on it, and leaping over is not any way to honor the bride and groom. In fact, it makes the toast more about you and your laughs than about them. Always remember that the point of this is to honor and entertain the bride & groom first, the crowd second, and yourself third.

With that soapbox lecture in mind, here are three promises you can make to both your BSF and the significant other to put their minds at ease and avoid having them all up in your shit about the speech. Call it a preemptive strike without showing your cards:

1. **I promise not to be downright mean:** It's well known that one of Google's (ever hear of them?) core company values is "Don't be evil." Same idea here. While I can't imagine intentionally being evil during a wedding toast, the barometer should be to avoid hurting any feelings. If something you say is funny and good natured, and someone takes offense, I have no sympathy for them. However, if you have an ax to grind with the bride, groom or somebody in the room and you think this is the perfect stage to knock them down a peg, that is being mean. There's no place for that in your toast, and the bride/groom will be very happy to hear you say that to them in advance.

2. **I promise not to be sexually suggestive to the point of discomfort.**

3. **I promise to limit my stories of drunken escapades.**

These three commitments take very little effort on your end to communicate to the bride and groom, and will put their minds at ease. After hearing this from your mouth (or from your fingers if it's an email/text), they are likely to leave you alone to write the toast as you see fit.

In rare cases, you may run into a bride or groom that is paranoid to the point that they'll demand to see your speech in advance. To this, I can't really help you other than to suggest that you either take a stand and refuse, reluctantly accept their demands, or hand them a dummy speech and once you get the mic, do your thang ☺.

The Big Finish

If there's one thing I know, it's that the best speeches, regardless of occasion, end on a high note. Like the final, high pitched piece of the opera where all the women hit that beautiful shriek and hold it for a minute straight. Wouldn't you love to leave your audience with a big smile and your aunts & uncles wiping their mouths with a handkerchief because their jaws were stuck open?

Here's how to make that happen.

Save your best story, your best joke, or your #1 most defining moment with the couple for the end. Simple enough. Deliver it with emotion like you never have before, then wait for the house to come down.

If you don't have a joke off the top of your head, spend some time thinking about it. If you are racking your brain for a finisher, google "inspirational quotes," brainstorm your BSF's favorite book or movie for a quote, or reserve your most outstanding memory of that person for now.

If you're still stuck, think about the structure of a movie. Most movies have an introduction, where characters are introduced and some kind of back story is presented. Then, a conflict or objective arises, which requires the characters to set in motion a series of events, or rising action. Then, these events lead to a defining point in the story, the climax. This is where the conflict is addressed head-on and usually resolved. Most movies don't end immediately after the climax, but everything else afterward is, well, anticlimactic.

The "denouement" represents the rest of the movie. Lingering plot strings are tied up and it's usually a peaceful time that either provides closure or teases more to come in the sequel. For your speech, the first four COGS lead up to the climactic moment, your Big Finish. After the Big Finish, your denouement is to offer one last thanks and ask everyone to raise their glasses. The audience will stay engaged through your whole speech if they sense that you're heading for a climax. Use the first four COGS to build toward your climax, then give the people what they want.

Another dinosaur. Who doesn't like dinosaurs?

PETE HONSBERGER

Here are a couple movie examples of the climax (The Big Finish):

- **Jurassic Park (since I've mentioned it already):** When it looks like all is lost for the family, and they are surrounded by raptors, the T-Rex busts in the building and starts a fight. They then use the distraction to escape.
- **Love Actually:** The climax begins at the school Christmas production that features children dressed as lobsters. In this movie, we get a bonus climax when the young boy, Sam, catches up with his crush seconds before she boards a plane to the United States.
- **The Patriot:** When Mel Gibson kills the evil British soldier, it's the last stand he needs to make before everything else just seems to fall into place. Almost immediately after this triumph, the movie shows America accepting the English surrender.
- **10 Things I Hate About You:** It all goes down on prom night. Bianca punches Joey and falls for Cameron. Kat finds out that Patrick has been paid to date her and storms off. Bianca punches Joey in front of everyone. I know this movie came out in 1999, but if you haven't seen it I urge you to do so.
- **Fight Club:** Edward Norton putting the gun in his mouth and pulling the trigger. After that moment, there is no more struggle. Only the falling of buildings while he and his girlfriend hold hands and watch.
- **Rudy:** When Rudy gets inserted into the football game. He makes the game's final tackle and is carried off the field by his teammates.
- **Wedding Crashers (of course I have to mention this movie):** Vince Vaughn punches Bradley Cooper, ending the threat of Zach "the Sack" to Owen Wilson. Additionally, it helps Rachel McAdams avoid marrying the wrong man.

All you need to find is what your climax will be. It might be a one-liner, like mine in my speech for my brother below. It might be a quote that is meaningful to you and your BSF. It might be a story that proves to you why the new marriage will be successful. It might be you painting a mental picture of what their life together will be. It might be a recap of your best memory of the past and present with your BSF. It might be an impression of your BSF or a mutual friend. It might be you acting out a scene from a movie or show that you both love. It might be a heartfelt message that leaves no dry eye in the house. It might be a physical prop that cracks people up. Or it might be something more creative that you concoct. Don't be held back by my suggestions.

Just find your climax, your sendoff, your Big Finish. Then ride off triumphantly into a sea of top-shelf drinks.

12

Presentation Matters

Note: If you're skipping ahead or picking chapters at random, this is a reminder that brother, sister, or friend has been abbreviated to BSF to save reading time and paper space. This small effort to go green just may save the world.

I'll be the first to admit I'm not the authority on men and women's style. And I haven't yet been featured in GQ, though I'll be sure to let you know when I am. For my sake, it's a good thing it doesn't take the Neil DeGrasse Tyson of style or the Susan B. Anthony of fashion to know that a strong on-site presentation of your toast will improve how it's received. Conversely, looking disheveled, muttering and mumbling, or staring at the floor during your speech will have a detrimental effect.

Look, writing a speech and giving a speech are different skill sets. Some of you are naturals at sitting down and crafting beautifully worded toasts. Some can't write for shit but have an innate ability to get up in front of others and shine. Your toast requires you to do both. "Thanks Captain Obvious," you're probably thinking, and for good reason.

Well, that's why I'm here. Follow these quick tips and you'll have a fighting chance:

- Stand up straight with your chest slightly out. You're up there for a reason and should be proud of it. Stand like you mean it.

- When you get the microphone, take three seconds to survey the crowd before you speak. This will build the intrigue in the room and have people hanging on what you're about to say. It also provides time for you to gather the thought of your first sentence.
- Look at the audience more than you look at your speech. It's fine to look down and read off your page. However, don't ignore the human life forces that are accompanying you in the room.
- Allow your audience to laugh. When you tell a joke or a funny story, insert a pause so people can get their chuckle on. Then, resume spitting your hot fire.
- Hold the microphone close enough to your mouth. A lot of people may tell you not to "swallow the mic," but I would rather you be too loud than not loud enough. Wedding reception venues have all kinds of different sound acoustics and you never know who will have a hard time hearing. Don't deprive anyone in the back of the room from hearing your toast.
- Regardless of what you say in the speech, remember to propose a toast at the end. "Raise your glasses in celebration of Cory and Topanga," or something to that effect.

If you feel that you need more resource on the presentation aspect of your toast, by all means pursue it. Body language, nonverbal, speech posture, etc. are all areas that you can learn more about. If not, following the aforementioned tips will get you eighty to ninety percent strong. You're getting so close to a home run speech that I can barely stand it!

13

Party of Two

What if you're not the one, but rather one of the two people selected from seven billion to stand at your BSF's right hand? A quick Wikipedia search doesn't give me the answers that I need about whether this "dual maid of honor/best man" phenomenon is a new trend or ancient tradition. Regardless of its historical timeline, however, it's happening a lot these days. And if you know this is how it will go down, you best prepare for it.

If you don't have a co-conspirator on the best man/maid of honor train, then feel free to skip this chapter. But do so at your own risk, as you'll never know what pop culture references and hilarious (ly stupid) asides you might miss!

Are you still with me? Great, because even if this isn't your situation right now, it could be someday. To ensure success and smoothgevity (new word made by me), you really only need to do three things.

1. **Reach out to the other guy/gal:** "I know, it's crazy right? But if it had to be two people I'm glad it's you and me," is how the conversation may go. Remember that you did nothing wrong and neither did your counterpart. This doesn't need to be a rivalry. Your BSF chose this path because he or she simply could not choose and wants to show equal love to both of you. Neither

of you released a "Burn Book," so any energy you spend feeling upset or slighted about this will be wasted.

2. **Decide the route you want to take with your toast:**

   a. Write your toast independent of the other best man/maid of honor, and there's absolutely nothing wrong about that. If your counterpart suggests that you tag team the speech but you'd rather just handle it on your own, that's your prerogative. Simply be polite when you break the news to the other person. Something like "That's a great idea, but I'd really like to give it a shot solo. I've always wanted to be in this position and I want to see how well I can do."

   That should do the trick. You can even add that you've already started writing your toast, or that you'd be willing to compare notes so the two don't overlap.

   b. Brainstorm, share notes and write two speeches together with the yang to your wedding yin. Then deliver them separately. This is the route I chose for Dan's wedding. While he didn't technically select a best man or a bridal party in general, he selected his friend John and I to both give toasts at the reception. We both wanted to give independent toasts that entertained the crowd and honored Dan and Kate.

   However, we didn't want the same stories, the same jokes, and the same content in both speeches. This actually could have happened because we grew up together and had so many shared experiences. To avoid this, we talked a few times in advance of the wedding weekend, sharing ideas for the speeches' jokes and structures. In fact, he had a bit in his toast about Dan personally sending him mail from his employer (a bank) requesting that he sign up for credit cards, which I thought was hilarious.

   This kind of common ground will help you complement your counterpart instead of stepping on toes. And if you don't know the other person very well, this is an awesome opportunity to connect with him or her and help prepare for a pair of toasts that will make the bride and groom beam with pride. If the fear of reaching out and talking with this person is too great, seek him or her out at the bachelor/bachelorette party after about six drinks when your courage is at an all-time high.

    c.   Tag-Team the speech. I've noticed this to be especially popular when two brothers or sisters are the co-best men/maids of honor. To do this right, you're going to want two microphones and a clear description of who talks when. As you will hear me say in the next chapter (Guest Speakers), multiple people on the microphone does not equal creative license to put on a twenty-minute show.

3. **Prepare, prepare, prepare, and don't apologize:** Remember when you were in school and your teacher or professor assigned group projects? There always seemed to be at least one group member that did no work and got the same grade as the rest of the group. This friggen kid either left early from every group meeting or didn't show up at all. But you and your team felt too guilty to say anything about it, or maybe it was because you heard that snitches get stitches.

    Well, the truth is that kid probably didn't feel great about himself either. And after a while, you likely learned to pay no mind to people that didn't carry their own weight. At some point you decided to finish the project, be proud of what you did, and enjoy the results you earned.

    The same goes for your wedding toast. Once you've reached out and offered to compare notes with your counterpart, your conscience is clean. Go about your preparation, incorporate lessons from any sources (hopefully this book is one) you've consulted, use the Dynamite Toast Checklist, and put together your best possible presentation.

    Whether or not your counterpart puts in as much work is not your problem. While it isn't a competition, that doesn't mean you need to keep the other person in mind throughout your entire preparation process. Getting a little dark and ominous here, Pete? Sorry. All I'm trying to say is that if you go first, and your counterpart starts his or her speech with "Well, I don't know how I'm going to follow that," you should be proud of the job you did rather than sympathetic to the other person. Knock your toast out of the park!

While I'm on the topic, beware of advance complaining from your counterpart about how he or she "Is such a bad writer," "can't think of anything," or "this is way too hard." This is a victim mentality and doesn't deserve your sympathy or validation. If you've been gracious enough to offer to help brainstorm, and you still hear this from your counterpart, simply tell them to either buy this book or shut up. There's a difference between humility and grasping for sympathy. Don't apologize for putting in the work and doing an unbelievable job for your BSF.

Guest Speakers

Guest speaker, exhibit A. (via Shrout Photography)

I'm almost afraid to offer this suggestion. Used as a supplement that adds value, impact and humor to the speech, it's a great idea. However, if a guest speaker is a crutch to lean on, this can go off the rails fast.

In a lot of cases, it's an appealing idea. I get that, and have been a part of it multiple times. If you're going to go down this road, however, keep a few things in mind:

- **Length:** More people involved in the speech does not mean the audience wants to listen for twice as long. If you have a guest, keep his or her participation to two minutes or less.
- **Location:** Where is this person going to come from? Will he or she walk over from the head table, the crowd, or bust out through the cake after hiding inside? Decide this in advance, as well as which microphone will be used and how that handoff will occur.
- **Impact:** Think about the punchline for this extra effort. Is your guest speaker a great friend that just didn't get selected as best man/maid of honor? Is it another brother/sister, or someone that uniquely knows something hilarious about your BSF? As long as this person knows the role and can add value in two minutes or less, by all means go for it.

I'm telling you, though, if you parade multiple people up to the microphone like witnesses at a trial, and your combined speech makes the other toast look like a 5K compared to an Ultramarathon, I will personally show up and unplug your mic. If this book gets big, who knows, maybe I'll make enough money to quit my job and travel the world attending random wedding receptions for fun. You never know where I might be, hanging by the bar, keeping a low profile in my blue Joseph A. Bank suit, watching you with a sharp eye as I vaguely explain my made-up backstory to your Uncle Dave.

Bring as much heat as you can. But remember, humans love eighty degrees and can't handle one hundred fifty. Make your impact, just don't burn retinas and crush ear drums with a half hour of guest speakers.

Take it from Here

As I write this passage, I'm on an airplane headed to a wedding. Part of the intrigue for me every time I attend a wedding is in the speeches. Will they make me laugh? Will there be an original approach that I never could have imagined? Or will the speeches be a speedbump in an otherwise fun day?

I know I've already said this, but truth is that there's no perfect layout of a wedding speech. Remember, I'd love for you to take away from this reading experience that your toast is a significant honor that deserves your thought and preparation. Right or wrong, I see a wedding as a momentous celebration where anyone invited is fortunate to be there.

I don't care if forty-some percent of marriages end in divorce. I don't care how much money people spend and whether it's worth it. And I don't give a shit about the total head count. Whether it's fifty people or five hundred, a wedding is one of the truly good days of our lives.

The way the bride and groom look at each other. The walk down the aisle and the way the groom's face lights up. The collection of friends and family and their awkward introductions to each other. The romance of the first dance. And the wide smiles that I see every time. Those are the priceless notes of music that make up the beautiful symphony that is a wedding.

You have a chance to write a few of those notes. And like a favorite song that has an unforgettable chorus, your toast can have a profound effect on others, especially those who matter most.

Grab the mic. You got this! (via Shrout Photography)

16

Dynamite Toast Checklist

If you've read this far, you probably trust what I'm saying to some extent. My intention in writing this book is to increase the quality of wedding toasts one person at a time, for the sake of the guests, the bride & groom, and YOU!

So trust me when I say, if you commit to following this checklist and the due dates, you WILL deliver an awesome speech that honors your loved ones, delights the crowd, and lives on beyond just that night *for good reasons!* Pretty much any success I've ever had is from setting some kind of goal and executing on that goal, regardless of how painful it gets.

If you're not into writing or public speaking, it's going to get painful. Trust me, you can do it. We're talking about a few hours of your life dedicated to this task. That's it. You can do it at home, at the office, a coffee shop, a park, or anywhere you want.

So without further ado, here is the Dynamite Toast Checklist. A simple, single-page version is available at the end of the chapter:

☐ **21 Days to Wedding:** Spend thirty minutes reflecting and jotting down notes about your BSF. If you're having writer's block, ask yourself these questions:
   a. What is the funniest thing about this person?
   b. When did the two of you meet?

c. What story or stories do you talk about most when you hang out?

d. Is there a moment with this person that sticks out to you as a defining point in your relationship?

e. What quirk(s) does he/she possess?

f. Why is he or she so important to you?

Put some of these into words and don't worry about complete sentences or having it in any sort of order.

☐ **18 Days to Wedding:** Spend thirty minutes arranging your notes into order. Refer to the Five CRUCIAL COGS (Chapter 6) for assistance in determining the order.

☐ **14 Days to Wedding:** Write a rough draft and let it sit for a day, or at least overnight.

If you're comfortable doing so, share the draft with a close friend or family member for reaction and feedback. If you do this, however, either swear this person to secrecy or don't let the speech out of your sight. Additionally, require that this person gives you at least three pieces of feedback about the draft. One of the three comments MUST be a criticism or recommendation of what you can do to make it better. This can't just be a rubber stamp.

☐ **7 Days (one week!) to Wedding:** Read all the way through your rough draft, preferably a printed copy, and make another round of changes.

a. Are there words, phrases or sentences that don't add any humor, impact or value to the speech? If so, cut those.

b. Is there anything missing? Do you need one more story, or perhaps something more inspiring? If so, think hard for a few minutes and challenge yourself to uncover something awesome to add.

c. Try to think objectively for a minute about what your reaction would be if someone else gave this speech.

☐ **4 Days to Wedding:** Read the toast aloud to yourself. I guarantee there will be things that looked good on paper but don't sound right when said out loud. Go ahead and make these revisions. You are so close to being ready!

☐ **2 Days to Wedding:** Reflect for a few minutes on the entire process.

    a.   Is there anything that has popped into your head the past few days that you simply must add to your toast?

    b.   You can now anticipate the reaction of the crowd, like where you will want to pause for laughter, raise your voice, etc. It may be helpful to even write "(Pause)" into areas of the speech, just as a reminder to take a beat and allow for reaction. In addition, you don't want to rush through what'll be a memorable moment.

    c.   Ensure that you have at least two copies of your toast. I highly recommend printing these on paper and putting them into two pockets in different pieces of clothing. Or, email it to yourself so you *know* the dog won't make it disappear. The absolute last thing you want is to be rushing around trying to find your speech between the ceremony and reception. If you decide to read from technology—which I don't recommend if you can avoid it—for the love of God, be sure you have plenty of juice in your cell phone or iPad.

    d.   Spend at least a few moments giving thanks for the responsibility you have. As I mentioned at the beginning of this book, you are the only person in the world chosen as the best man/maid of honor for your BSF.

☐ **Wedding Day:** By this point you've done all the heavy lifting. You're prepared. You've done more than the vast majority of people in your position. Although it may be difficult because you're so excited, relax and have some fun!

MY PERSONAL DYNAMITE SPEECH CHECKLIST

☐ *21 Days to Wedding: Date_____Complete (Yes / No) _____*
   a. Spend thirty minutes in reflection about your BSF
   b. Take notes and record memories in no particular order

☐ *18 Days to Wedding: Date_____Complete (Yes /No) _____*
   a. Spend thirty minutes arranging stories and notes into order
   b. Refer to the Five CRUCIAL COGS for help

☐ *14 Days to Wedding: Date_____Complete (Yes /No) _____*
   a. Write a rough draft
   b. If you are comfortable, share this draft with someone you trust

☐ *7 Days to Wedding: Date_____Complete (Yes /No) _____*
   a. Read through rough draft and make any necessary changes
   b. Recommendation is to read the draft out loud from a printed version

☐ *4 Days to Wedding: Date_____Complete (Yes /No) _____*
   a. Second read-through out loud
   b. Put yourself in the audience's shoes and anticipate their reaction

☐ *2 Days to Wedding: Date_____Complete (Yes /No) _____*
   a. Add in any last-minute ideas or 2:00am epiphanies
   b. Make sure you have two copies printed (or saved electronically) and ready

☐ *Wedding Day: Date_____Complete (Yes /No) _____*
   a. Relax and enjoy the experience. You earned it.
   b. Remember to finish with "So raise your glasses for…"

17

Kate and Dan's Toast

I've referred to this speech several times already, so here it is in its entirety. This responsibility, in the Fall of 2012, was ultimately the catalyst for *Don't Burn Your Toast*. I had always been interested in telling a compelling story in front of a crowd. This experience, however, was addicting.

You be the judge whether you think it was entertaining, compelling, or any good at all. For me, it was a pleasure to brainstorm, write, rehearse and perform (and it helped that I had an eight-hour drive for rehearsal time). After that first moment, I've paid close attention to every wedding toast I've seen since. I had a taste of being part of the whole process, and became attracted to helping anyone else make theirs a big success.

Without weddings, love, and your willingness to read this book and put in the work to create a killer toast, none of this would be possible.

Turn the page for the full speech…

"Good evening everyone. I am Dan's younger brother Pete. Many of you I already know, some I have yet to meet.

Dan and Kate, thank you so much for the chance to speak on this very special occasion...By the way, I call first dance.

I've looked up to Dan ever since I've had sight, he was always bigger than me, and he was always right.

Being the oldest of four boys couldn't have been an easy thing. But in a house full of hyenas, Dan was the lion king.

I remember building traps in the basement when we were all kids, and how that came to an end when mom tripped on a bunch of well-placed mini bowling pins...sorry Mom.

But some of my best memories are days playing running-bases in the yard, or nights in our bedrooms trading baseball cards.

Or when the four of us would sleep in the same room on Christmas Eve night, or all the basketball games in the driveway, the video game tournaments, even the fights.

Dan's been an outstanding big brother, I couldn't ask for any more. Though he did once try to build a campfire in his bedroom and burned a hole in the floor (pause for laughter).

But any time I had questions or problems as a kid, Dan was there to help me through it. And when I took all the blame for breaking our neighbor's window, (get louder) hey, I was glad to do it!

Dan's been and will be a life-long brother, mentor, and friend to Mark, John, and me, and that will never end.

When he moved from Ohio to Richmond, we were all sad to see him leave. But he had opportunities to chase, and success to achieve.

Of course, his move to Virginia has led him to Kate. Whether by chance, luck, a love of the 80s, or fate.

And for the entire time I've seen the two of them together, bright green has been their grass, sunny has been their weather.

I'm proud of Dan, and really happy to officially welcome Kate to our family. You know, it's kind of funny. Dan's nickname growing up was "the Bear," and this Bear, has found his honey."

My three brothers and I before the wedding.

Write Your Toast

Now you've read the book, or at least some of it. This is where the rubber meets the road. In the following pages you'll find space and opportunity to jot down ideas, inside jokes, memories, stories, thoughts and musings to prepare for your toast. By all means, mark this section up. Make it look like damn high school yearbook.

Thank you for the commitment you've made to appropriately honoring your BSF. Remember, however, it may not all come pouring out of you at once. You may want to quit after your first attempt at brainstorming and resort back to waiting until the day before the wedding to throw something together.

But you won't. You already knew it wouldn't be easy. That's been well documented in this book. You've already made the decision to be a cut above the majority of wedding toasts, and I'm holding you to that standard. If you're beat down, think about your BSF, think about the significant other, and think about the wedding audience. Think about your opportunity to make an impression, an impact, a positive dent in the world.

If you need to, take a ten-minute break anytime you get stuck. Stand up, walk around, or get a drink. Then get your hind parts back in front of your computer or flip back to these final pages to write. For the brainstorming portion of your toast (between Day 21 and Day 14 before the wedding), structure is not as important as volume. Get as many ideas out there as possible. Refer to the Dynamite Toast Checklist for every leg of the writing process.

The following pages align with the checklist. Whether you follow the exact order I recommend is up to you. The important thing is to do the work. Henry Ford once said "Thinking is the hardest work there is, which is probably the reason why so few engage in it." Well, you are one of the few. It's GO TIME.

Good luck. We're all counting on you.

30-MINUTE BRAINSTORM:
REFLECT ON YOUR BSF AND SCRIBBLE SOME NOTES

_____

_____

_____

_____

_____

_____

_____

_____

_____

_____

_____

_____

_____

_____

30-MINUTE BRAINSTORM (CONTINUED):
REFLECT ON YOUR BSF AND SCRIBBLE SOME NOTES

_____

_____

_____

_____

_____

_____

_____

_____

_____

_____

_____

_____

THE FIVE CRUCIAL COGS:
THE OPENER

_____

_____

_____

_____

_____

_____

_____

_____

_____

_____

_____

_____

THE FIVE CRUCIAL COGS:
HONORING THE PAST

_____

_____

_____

_____

_____

_____

_____

_____

_____

_____

_____

_____

THE FIVE CRUCIAL COGS:
PRESENT AND FUTURE

THE FIVE CRUCIAL COGS:
THE SIGNIFICANT OTHER

THE FIVE CRUCIAL COGS:
THE BIG FINISH

_____

_____

_____

_____

_____

_____

_____

_____

_____

_____

_____

_____

YOUR COMPLETE TOAST:
ROUGH DRAFT

_____

_____

_____

_____

_____

_____

_____

_____

_____

_____

_____

_____

CONGRATULATIONS!!

OH AND ONE LAST THING...NOW YOU CAN CELEBRATE

Raise your glasses.

THE END

Acknowledgments

For anyone that has helped make this project possible, I cannot thank you enough. To Jenna, the love of my life. Thank you for your constant support, encouragement, and the kicks in the butt to keep going. To my parents, Jim and Kathy, for the help and kind words along the way. To my brothers and sister-in-law, thanks for being there to bounce ideas with. Special thanks to Dan and Kate Honsberger for giving me my first wedding toast opportunity and providing huge inspiration for this book.

To Brian and Carli Velbeck for the ideas and permission to refer to your wedding, which was amazing. To Rich and Katie Velbeck, who put up with a loud interruption in their best men toast. To Matt Huml, who tossed me some incredibly helpful feedback...I'm counting on you to buy copies of this if no one else will.

To John Lee Dumas and Kate Erickson for *The Freedom Journal*, which was a catalyst for this project. To the TFJ Community, I am honored to have completed a goal alongside you.

A sincere thank you to anyone who read and shot holes in my first draft, including Lindsay Foster, Leigh McDermott, Vincent Pugliese, Jenna, Mom, Dan, and Kate.

Lastly, thanks to you for reading. This investment will pay huge dividends in your toast. And if it doesn't, I'll buy you a drink.

Made in the USA
Lexington, KY
27 December 2017